Drew,

The work you + your
team does makes an impact
on so many. It is a privilege
to work together.

HOW COLLEGE HAS DESTROYED
A GENERATION OF EMPLOYEES
AND HOW TO FIX IT.

SAM CAUCCI

FOR THE COACHES, FRIENDS, TEAMMATES AND FAMILY THAT HAVE PLAYED A PART IN THE TRAINING THAT HAS PREPARED ME FOR THE CHALLENGES I FACE EVERYDAY. AND TO, OF COURSE, MY MOTHER.

Contents

INTRODUCTION

"IF A MAN TAKES NO INTEREST IN PUBLIC AFFAIRS, WE ALONE DO NOT CONDEMN HIM AS QUIET BUT CONDEMN HIM AS USELESS."

PERICLES
GREEK STATESMAN

So here I was in the boardroom at a major New York City area university surrounded by the Dean, the Director of Career Services and several key professors, all the people who play a major role in creating the university's curriculum. The Dean was seated at the head of the table.

I was there to present my plan on how to bring a sales and customer service curriculum addition to the university and I was getting ready to begin. I put up my power point deck and got started.

I explained the realities of opportunities in today's workforce. I shared feedback I heard from employers about what they want from graduates. I began to present on why teaching sales and customer service principles to students is important - a subject in which fewer than 1 percent of universities offer a major or even a minor. And quickly I was interrupted by the Dean.

"That's not our job," said the Dean.

Me, a bit shocked, "What do you mean?".

"It is not our job to prepare students for the workforce," he said. "It's not our job to spend time on customer service or sales training. It's the responsibility of the employer to do that. It is our responsibility to educate."

I was shocked. And frankly I was disturbed. I had worked with colleges in the past for a number of reasons. From hiring interns to guest lecturing in classes, I had been very active in trying to stay connected to local universities knowing that our community is stronger when companies and universities stay engaged to create opportunities for young workers. Sharing my experiences with classrooms and professors had become routine. And I expected the point of view of all universities to be to constantly find ways to create more value for the students that are spending so much to attend.

As I look back, this Dean's response really didn't shock me. It pissed me off.

Recently I sat in a different conference room. This time at a major corporation which primarily hires young talent right out of universities, a major corporation that spends a great deal of its human resources budget on recruiting, interviewing and hiring new employees to step into their company. And, in that presentation - one in which I was promoting tools to help better train and better prepare employees, I was interrupted again. This time by the CEO.

The CEO said, "Training things that our people should already know is not our job. If they can't figure it out then they won't last working here."

A job means so much more than a paycheck. A person that has a job has a vehicle to deliver their purpose. And when properly prepared they feel that sense of purpose fulfilled. People being proud of the work they do in their job and in turn doing well at their job - should be an important goal for all organizations. People that are prepared not only do better work, they also deliver a better experience to customers and to their organization. People that are prepared for their job, and are empowered and confident in the work they do everyday, become better spouses and even better parents. They are more likely to give back to the community and they are less likely to be incarcerated.

See, a job is so much more than a paycheck. And it is our job as employers, teachers, politicians, policy makers, lawmakers, parents, students and employees - to ensure that our people can succeed in their job.

This Book

I am not a writer. And becoming an expert in an area such as workforce training and development was something of an accident. On my journey in several businesses I have gained tremendous experience finding, training and coaching people. I have worked at all ends of the training spectrum. From re-training young workers coming out of college in New Jersey on how to use email and PowerPoint correctly, something that is somehow always left out of a well rounded college education, to working with leading companies like Madison Square Garden and over 100 other companies to re-design training and development programs to improve employee success. These experiences have given me a front row seat to observe how the problems I will address here have emerged.

A few years ago I was in a coffee shop on a trip to San Francisco. Sitting at the counter sending emails I eavesdropped on the interaction of the cashier and the manager in what appeared to be a trial by fire initial training during a primetime morning rush. Clearly aggravated at not understanding the manager's directives on how to operate the register and manage the flow of orders, the employee became frozen. You know that look when you have no idea what is happening in Calculus class so you stare at the board and pray for the bell to ring? This employee had zoned out. She was clearly not understanding what was happening and was a bit embarrassed that her struggle was being put on display for so many customers. And now for the best part. The manager, putting years of leadership training into action, responds, "This is how I got trained. You will be fine."

It is debilitating to our society and workforce when workers come out of a university and step into their first role without the tools to be successful. And it drains the energy from a worker when they get hired and receive the minimum in formalized training to prepare them for their work.

This book started as a simple idea and grew into a keynote that I have delivered dozens of times across the country to rooms full of people ranging from educators to corporate business leaders. In it we will explore the problem that we currently face in regards to the future of the people that drive our workforce. We will look at the problem that has been fueled by four key groups, Educators, Employers, Employees, and Lawmakers. All have played a critical role in creating this crisis.

I will also provide a few thoughts regarding the solutions to correct this problem, solutions that I have made my career goal to see implemented. That I have made it my career goal to address.

And yes, this book is a bit of a tirade. Just bear with me. The facts I have unearthed should shock you. But I hope my thoughts will impress upon you the need for action. And regardless of the role you play in our workforce it is important you understand where we are so that you can help to right our track forward.

Let's go.

165 million jobs
in the U.S. in 2015

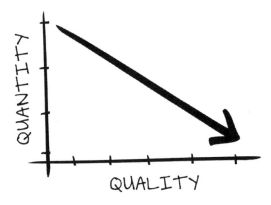

┌labor participation┐ *is* **UP**
└─ (QUANTITY) ─┘

but

the ┌number of skilled workers┐ *is* **DOWN**
└─── (QUALITY) ───┘

The State of the Workforce

Today, we have a problem.

And to understand that problem we must understand where we are, and really understand what is going on below the surface. Not just focusing on one part of the issue or being swayed by any one voice or news source. It is only then that we can really look at how we are going to craft a solution.

Some 55 million jobs are going to open to the present workforce by the year 2020. These jobs consist mostly of opportunities created due to the retirement of baby boomers, as well as new employees coming into a workforce where jobs have begun to return.

Today in America there are 165 million jobs. Coming out of the recent recession labor participation is up; however, the number of skilled workers is down.

The challenges we face have been discussed and debated by everyone from leading economists to politicians across the globe. In July 2014, The White House released a report, 'Ready to Work', in which they identified three core problems at the heart of our current workforce challenges. They are:

1. Universities need to do a better job aligning with the workforce to understand what universities need to teach.

2. Companies are having a harder time finding skilled workers.

3. Students are delaying and are more hesitant to invest in ongoing education because they are unsure about their potential return on investment.

Our economy is not plagued by a lack of jobs. It's plagued by the under productive. And the under production of prepared university graduates is doing major damage to our economy, and is one of the greatest threats to our ability to successfully emerge from the recent recession.

Consider: According to the Economic Policy Institute, 53.6 percent of millennials are either unemployed or underemployed. This is a generation that is entering their post college career at a very challenging moment. They are told the job market is bleak. They carry more student debt then any generation before them. And over 16 percent of these new workers will still be paying down college debt when they're 50 years old.

Yet the jobs are there, often going unfilled. Talk to companies and 39 percent of CEO's say they cannot find skilled workers for the jobs they have available. Companies want to hire and they need to hire. But, they are hesitant to hire. Nervous about the quality of talent they will get, companies have grown more unwilling to take on the task of training an unqualified millennial.

So again it comes back to training. And the big question is, "Whose job is it?"

Unemployment numbers are traditionally broken out into two categories: long-term unemployed and short-term unemployed. Long-term unemployed are those employees who have been out of the workforce for 6 months or longer. And with fewer job opportunities available to college graduates, they have delayed the start of their career, essentially joining the ranks of the long-term unemployed right out of college.

Understanding the difference between long-term and short-term unemployed is important because as recent research from Harvard Business Review shows, if you are a long-term unemployed worker it can take you 3.5 times longer to find a job than a short-term unemployed worker. For every 10 applications a short-term unemployed worker submits, a long-term unemployed worker has to submit 35. That's a lot of time to spend on those pain in the ass job search sites.

Today, our under productivity of labor is doing more damage than ever before. When the great recession recedes completely we will be left with a labor force that has a massive misalignment between the skills they have and the demands of a 21st Century workforce.

I repeat, "Whose job is it to fix this?"

THE PROBLEM

"EDUCATION IS THE MOST POWERFUL
WEAPON THAT YOU CAN USE
TO CHANGE THE WORLD."

NELSON MANDELA
PRESIDENT OF SOUTH AFRICA

The College Problem

Failing Grades

In all, $1.1 trillion in American tax dollars were spent on education in 2014. Nearly $600 billion comes from educational investment in primary, secondary and post-secondary education. And close to $400 billion is spent on corporate training programs.

Those are big numbers, proof that real money is being spent. But how it is being spent is the bigger concern.

In 2014, US government sent **$16 Billion** in aid to students at 4 year colleges - who eventually graduated less than 1/3 of students within 6 years.

In 2014, the U.S. government sent $16 billion in aid to students at four-year colleges that had graduated just under one third of their students in six years. It just doesn't add up. It just doesn't make any sense.

Meanwhile, the public's trust in education is slipping. Turn on the TV and you're apt to see a documentary challenging the true value of a college education. Open a newspaper and you can read about the 20 Atlanta educators who doctored tests and cheated for their students to get bonuses and bump up their students' scores on standardized tests.

Maybe its time we step back and challenge how we are spending that $1.1 trillion.

According to the former US Secretary of Labor Robert Reich, we are experiencing a time in which nearly 43 states have reduced funding for education and all 50 have increased the cost of tuition. Decisions are being made that more and more do not have the best interest of students in mind. Decisions are being made to increase enrollment and tuition, but are not always focused on increasing spending to better improve the quality of education.

The value of a college education is pretty simple to figure out. In an up or down vote I would vote that a college education is valuable, and a majority of the research backs me up. An individual that goes to college and completes a four-year degree will earn over $1 million more in their lifetime compared to one who does not. But there is more to this question that we will address later.

So I am sure that we can all agree that college is valuable. It's of value to our society and it's of value to the students who attend a university. But let's dive deeper. Let's ask ourselves: "at what cost?". And at what point is the cost too much?

The amount of college loan debt today is astronomical. Since 2007, college loan debt has doubled to $1.2 trillion, and the number of college loans and grants that have been issued has increased by 50 percent. College tuition has outpaced inflation for three decades. The average college graduate carries a debt load of $15,000 after graduation - a number that shackles college students and in many ways irrationally affects decision-making about a post-graduate career. It strengthens fear and insecurity at a time when these young people simply cannot afford to enter the workforce afraid. The reality of the job search process alone is enough to do this, not withstanding the additional weight of a loan payment.

We must tackle this issue and find ways to create an environment where people can pursue an affordable education. And affordable should not mean a drop in quality. Affordable should mean a cost that is fair. And the customer (the student!) must be assured that their skill will be improved, their knowledge will be increased, and they will be in a better position to succeed in the workforce.

So yes, we look at millennials and we notice that in their movement to enter the workforce they face great problems and troubles. But let's not forget there is an entire generation right behind them - Generation Z - and they are coming up fast.

Look closely at Generation Z and you'll see it's essentially like the millennial generation - only worse in their weakest areas.

It's a generation that grew up much differently than earlier generations. I know when I grew up I spent hours outside playing sports and time talking on the phone. This generation has grown up in a time where exploring the neighborhood until dark is not so common anymore and running over your cell phone minutes has been replaced by surging text message plans. This new generation is not getting the opportunities to screw up and learn from their mistakes, and they are not getting the communication practice that is critical to the development of skills they will need later in life.

It is a group that is believed to lack high levels of situational awareness and is being labeled as socially awkward. Their lack of experiences has created a critical gap that affects their ability to form the habits that develop skills necessary to succeed.

False Advertising

In 2015, scary things began to surface about several large for-profit schools. Take, for example, the large for-profit education company Corinthian Colleges, with more than 16,000 students. A federal investigation found that Corinthian in its pursuit of selling students on their programs, had falsified job placement numbers, graduation rates and the success of their programs. Investigators have found that since 2010, Corinthian Colleges has placed over 947 false advertisements in everything from newspapers to magazines to billboards claiming inflated job placement rates.

It gets worse.

Corinthian, at its peak, had 120 colleges, nearly 110,000 students, and was valued at $1.4 billion. It has been a long fall. The college's infractions resulted in the closing of 30 campuses in which over 42 percent of students were within 6 months of graduation. The economic impact was tens of thousands of wasted dollars to so many young people who had invested so much to attain so little.

And Corinthian Colleges is not unique, and it's not the only for-profit school being investigated by the U.S. government and the Department of Education. Devry University, Kaplan, University of Phoenix and nearly a dozen others are being investigated for the same allegations.

The colleges and universities that are responsible for preparing people for the workforce are rapidly losing the trust and faith of their customers. At a time when people are questioning whether an investment in their education will produce the return on investment and skills they need to qualify for jobs, the very institutions that we trust to provide those answers are cheating and misleading the people.

43 states
have reduced funding for education

& all 50 states
have increased the cost of tuition.

And still, it gets worse.

According to the "Wall Street Journal," if every Corinthian College student requested forgiveness for their loans it would cost the American taxpayer nearly $3.5 billion. The students who were misled and spent their time, energy, and money to receive an education are entitled to a refund. But the Department of Education is trying to find a way around this happening. In an effort to minimize losses that would result from forgiving these student loans, the federal government is choosing to protect big college businesses over students. Recent claims for forgiveness of college loans by former students has been met with resistance by the Department of Education.

Instead of choosing a path to responsibly handle these claims in a manner that is timely and efficient for students, they have created an apparatus that more often challenges requests instead of helping these students. Only more to deal with for students that now must make a decision on what their next step is with a transcript that is incomplete and may not even have much value. It was their choice to grant for-profit schools and loan agencies the tax dollars to support their infrastructure - and when evidence shows that these organizations did not operate in good faith to their customers it is the federal government that is cheating the people. At Corinthian College, over 90 percent of its revenue comes from American tax dollars.

It is the mortgage crisis of 2008 all over again, only this time it is on the backs of college students and especially upon the backs of low-income individuals in pursuit of the American dream in the very place we tell them to look - a college or university. It's just another story of the attempts by the federal government and the Department of Education to effectively oversee and manage schools. And it has resulted in failure.

The Bill

Over 40 million Americans currently owe nearly $1.2 trillion in college loan debt. Trillion. With a 'T'.

That is a problem.

Today, 8 million Americans are currently in default on their college loan, and 1 out of every 3 students will be in default at some point during their loan term. This problem can become a nightmare very quickly. And while the impact might make headlines in the form of the stock market or the closure of several universities, I can assure you the impact on the individuals in default is much greater. Being jobless, in default, and unable to pay for the education they pursued can cripple families, communities, cities, states and beyond.

These are the people that are harassed daily.

A 2015 investigation by the Federal Consumer Bureau found examples of student loan specialists charging illegal fees, misleading borrowers about minimum monthly payments, processing payments in a way that maximizes fees and harassing borrowers with late night and early morning calls against federal regulations.

What a great business model!

The Corporate Problem

Welcome to the Real World

Companies invest in a variety of methods to train their people. Some invest in robust on-line learning platforms. Some even add lengthy initial on-boarding programs to excite new workers and ensure people start off on the right foot. And some have systems in place to ensure that there is a presence of ongoing training and continued education. But, unfortunately, such companies are in the minority.

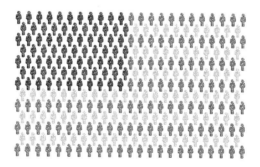

Over *40 million Americans* currently owe nearly
$1.2 trillion
in college loan debt.

Most companies have weak and under-funded training programs that do not have the best interests of the worker in mind. Some subscribe to a 'train and pray' model where there is a great deal of initial training and no ongoing reinforcement. You sink or you swim.

Others have done away with entry-level paid positions altogether in favor of 100 percent commission roles, unpaid internships or independent contractor positions. This is a response by corporations who are trying to mitigate their risk and in a way argue that the skill level of workers does not meet their needs.

The result of poor training practices is turnover. It is an outcome that is debilitating to our economy in a post-recession environment. The costs of turnover can be very expensive to a company. For a company today the cost to replace an entry level worker is between 30-50 percent of the employee's salary, and the cost can be over 400% for a high level worker. In certain high-demand roles the results of poor training is shocking. In a recent study of entry-level sales representatives, the management consulting firm Accenture found that 9 out of 10 reps will turn over within their first two years on the job.

Whose job is it to make sure they stick?

Follow the Leader

Managers need to be better prepared. We live in a time today in which the standard practice is to take the best employee, often the highest performing sales or service rep, and promote that person into management roles.

Our core focus must be on training and development, growing and building, strengthening and expanding the skill of people. The last thing we should be doing is promoting our top employees into management and leadership roles solely because they excel at the functions of the job they are in.

Within most sales organizations this practice is like wild fire. It has become standard practice to take the best sales rep and make them the sales manager. The reality is that just because you're a good employee, does not mean you are going to be a great manager. Managers that were promoted strictly on their performance are likely to coach their people to perform their job in the same fashion that they did and fail to take into account that different employees with different personalities and different basic skill-sets can be successful in ways that maybe that manager wasn't.

And the natural tendency to promote people into management based solely on their success as an employee without giving them the training and tools to be great managers, means front line-employees will not get the coaching they need and deserve. This practice is also not in the best interest of the manager that is promoted. These people are left often without guidance and are also at risk of failure.

There is a better approach.

Instead, we should promote and grow the employees within our organizations that have the best natural talent, foundation and skill-set at growing, coaching and leading.

If we want to ensure that employees grow and maximize their talent in the roles they are in we must make sure we put the people in management roles that have the best skill set to grow, lead, and develop others. A management job should not be used as a trophy or a reward to an employee who happens to be a top performer.

Stick to this old practice and we are not fixing the problem. We are only increasing the likelihood that front line employees will not get trained. They will become disgruntled and they will quit.

The Employee Problem

Internships are Broken

The goal of an internship, at the end of the day, is to prepare people for the workforce. The reality is companies are using internships in a totally different way.

Whether it is as free help or to actually create a pipeline to convert interns into full time employees, companies are not investing time, energy, resources and money to ensure that the interns that they hire get the necessary training and a valuable experience.

Universities are also at fault.

If you look across the 2,000+ universities today you will find that a wide array of them approach internships very differently. Some have requirements that more often than not hurt the intern if they are strictly adhered to. An example of this would be maximum hour requirements that some universities place on interns to discourage them from working full-time. When a student applies for an internship with a company, in today's market, you cannot realistically limit the amount of time and energy that they commit to the internship without damaging their chance of success.

So why do companies even bother with internships. For a few reasons:

1. **Free Labor.** They need additional labor that they otherwise would not (or could not) have paid for. About 50 percent of internships are paid, 50 percent are unpaid.

2. **Give Back.** They want to give back - knowing that it is also their responsibility to be proactive in helping young people.

3. **Recruiting.** They believe in the value of bringing in young and fresh talent because they believe in the prospect of potentially hiring the best candidates into a full-time paid position in the future.

Too often, students treat internships like an entitlement. Like part of the curriculum. Like something that companies are supposed to give them.

The only way the quality of internships will improve is if both sides of the relationship invest more time, energy and effort into the experience. Companies have to make sure the internship program is valuable for the student. And students must learn to treat internships as a full-time job.

A few years ago I received an email from a past intern. This intern had completed a 3-month internship program with me in which he was engaged in the first month, a low performer in the second month and laidback in the third month. It was a progression in which his slow fall would result in no formal recommendations in the future. The email I received surprised me.

Sam,

Heard your company is hiring. Its truly amazing how i remember sitting next you and you had your company in the baby stages and now look at it...i got an email for a job opportunity! In all honesty I just wanted to let you know that when i interned for you, i did slack, mainly because i wasn't being paid and it was senior year of college...but come on, can you blame me? At least i entertained you. I did learn a lot of important lessons from just talking to you, probably learned a lot more in 3 months with you than 4 years at college. I just wanted to let you know if you actually do consider me for a position, I know sounds scary, I understand this is your company, this is your child, you worked very hard to build it into what it is today, Hope to hear back from you soon...

This email angers me because he could have done better. He could have worked harder. He had the skill to do it and missed the opportunity. The above email unfortunately is not the exception, it is the norm. It happens way too often today with people entering the workforce without the necessary guidance to do the simple things well...like compose an email. Internships are a full time position. Employees need to approach them as such.

So a few things have to happen.

Students can no longer approach an internship as if they are volunteers and doing the company a favor. They must hold the internship experience in high regard, at the same level as a full-time paid position. Otherwise the entire experience will be wasted.

And then they need to work and deliver throughout the course of the internship. They must go above and beyond. They need to be able to put something on their resume that looks better than just 'References available upon request'.

At the same time, colleges need to ease up on requirements. Placing heavy restrictions on how many hours a student can work holds them back. It holds them back from taking full advantage of the opportunity and from gaining real experience, and that doesn't make sense. An intern should be free to do as much work as they want in order to gain the experience they need. Period.

Hey colleges! If you want to do anything why don't you require companies to provide you with their 12-week training curriculum for their internship program. Make this a requirement for qualification as an approved internship provider instead of having them submit a lousy 1-pager that overviews what they think their internship program delivers. Do this instead of setting maximum requirements, and instead focus on the real goal which is to provide a student with a quality experience that includes networking, meeting new people and building relationships. Which is what an internship should be all about.

Companies, meanwhile, need to spend more time designing their internship programs in a way that creates a win-win opportunity/experience for the student and the organization. Yet many organizations neglect to even think through the design of their internship program. Is it 12-weeks? 16-weeks?

What do we expect of them? What do we want the students to take away?

Some just throw students into the fire, creating a chaotic intern experience which leaves the student upset and the organization at a loss because they spent months training someone who is now gone and who failed to excel at any project for that organization.

We need to impress upon students that the goal isn't to collect 3 credits. The goal is not to get the job. The goal is not to hit an hour requirement.

The goal of the internship is to gain essential experiences, experiences that are impossible to get in a classroom.

Also, many students only pursue paid internships, and that's a mistake. They should be encouraged to consider unpaid opportunities as well. Knowing that the most valuable experiences sometimes come with no compensation.

In the end, internships fail because of a disconnect between businesses and academia. It is a disconnect that hurts the people that are working hard to prepare themselves to enter the workforce. We cannot continue to do the same thing and expect a different result. I am tired of listening to companies complain that workers don't have the right skills and students complain that nobody is helping them. It needs to be fixed.

And that is our job.

Demand Training

The job training process for interns and full time employees should be a great experience. Unfortunately, most employers don't put the time and energy into it to ensure that they create a high quality program.

We can't give students a **1980s** education and expect them to be prepared for a **21st century** workforce.

The relationship between a company and its employee should be one where there is shared responsibility. Where employees are responsible to work hard to prepare for their work and where companies work hard to ensure that their people have all the resources need to succeed. If you get a job, the expectation is you are going to get the training and experiences that will shape or form the skills you need.

It is the responsibility of the people to demand the training they deserve. Whether in an internship or in a full time position, true reform is not going to happen if employees continue to sit back and allow companies to provide sub-par training.

A revolution must occur. And it must start with the people on the job. You must demand it.

The Lawmaker Problem

Creating Jobs

In 1930, John Maynard Keynes made a statement. Keynes, an important economist in American history and founder of modern day macroeconomic theory, said the average American should work 3 hours per day. Well, I think that number has changed.

Today, there are roughly 141 million workers in the US (112 million in the private sector and 29 million in government jobs). These workers are the lifeblood of our economy. And it is the responsibility of our legislators to ensure an environment in which current workers can thrive and in which new jobs are created.

Unfortunately, in the time after the Great Recession, we have experienced an era in which we have been misled. Consistent focus on the unemployment rate has disguised the under-production of skilled workers in return for the excuse that there are no jobs available. This false storyline has left us in a position where as the unemployment rate has gone down an entire workforce has emerged with critical skill gaps.

A key component of job creation is a concept called "knowledge spillover," the sharing of knowledge and skills that takes place in a community. The premise is that the presence of more skilled people in a city, especially those that are college educated, will result in more and better jobs for the less skilled. The earnings of a worker with a high school education rises over 7 percent as the share of college graduates in that geographic area increases by 10 percent.

Government has the responsibility to ensure that it encourages an environment in which jobs are created. You might find that the way to create jobs is not what you have been told on the 24-hour news channels. It is not always as simple as lowering business taxes. The creation of sustainable jobs occurs when our educational system is aligned with the skills needed by today's employers, when people can access the right education, and companies are motivated to hire.

The question is: How do we help communities that are stuck with the wrong mix of jobs and skills?

Tackling this problem is where the people that earn our votes can earn their worth.

Internships are Important

Internships are under attack today. Many people in government believe that we need to rethink the internship model because it is creating an environment that kills jobs for willing workers. This claim is false.

In all, 1.3% of the nearly 175 million workers today are interns. These interns make up a part of the workforce that would otherwise not be a paid position. They play a vital role in the labor economy of creating a pipeline - a segway - between unemployed and employed. Internships also allow people the opportunity to gain different experiences. In some cases even allowing individuals the opportunity to experience different jobs in different industries then maybe their major or existing skill-set had pointed them towards.

In the sports industry there are over 500 sports management programs in a space that overwhelmingly drives students toward a vey narrow amount of job positions. When you have situations like this occurring, we need to make sure that we create as many opportunities as possible to help students diversify the opportunities they may be interested in. Not everybody is going to be the General Manager of a major sports franchise. There is no way you know what you want to do for the rest of your life when you are 18-20 years old. We need to stop impressing this upon students as a benchmark.

We must diversify the learning experience beyond the cookie cutter approach that occurs with most academic tracks. It is unethical to reduce opportunities for students to expand their horizons...if anything we should make the pursuit of different experiences more of a requirement. Internships essentially allow the labor force to think outside the box.

There are many people in Washington that believe internships kill jobs, and that companies are reducing paid full-time employee positions in favor of cheaper intern labor. Many states are working to create tighter regulations around companies that hire interns, without realizing the damage that the move has on younger workers. And the further damage that such regulations would have on companies of all sizes that would now be forced to rethink their hiring strategies.

Now in some cases it may be true that a small business or mid-size corporation decides to shift responsibilities to an intern's job description, instead of a full-time staff member. In these cases, lawmakers should ask, "Why are employers doing that?"

And I believe that the small amount of jobs that may be lost to interns are lost because some companies are too greatly challenged when it comes to their own internal approach to staff training. These companies already see staff training as expensive, and now with employees that have weaker skill-sets entering the workforce they see it as even more so. This has left some companies to believe that they can mitigate their risk by trusting interns over full time employees.

A truth is that in most cases, if workers would be prepared for those jobs then they would step into those jobs and excel. And if they were excelling at those jobs then companies would pay them!

In sales, the notion that companies prefer an intern over a productive full-time employee is ridiculous.

Companies want workers that produce. Companies want employees that are successful. Companies want employees that generate revenue. And when they generate revenue they create an environment where they validate further investment in that worker.

There is no benefit that a company can glean by reducing full-time jobs in favor of unpaid internships - other than to mitigate the risk of paying somebody who doesn't produce.

The College Connection

Employment prospects for college graduates are grim, with more than 40 percent ending up with a job that didn't even require a college degree. And while recently the earnings of college graduates have improved, it is more a function of them swiping jobs from displaced high school graduates. Today, about 60 percent of parking lot attendants have some college education.

Meanwhile, default rates on large college loans are a major issue. A recent Department of Labor report found that 11 percent of graduates from a four-year college in 2011 had already defaulted by 2013. Within two years these graduates already found themselves in a position to not be able to fulfill their loan obligation. If this continues to grow and widen, this strain will impact people far beyond these 11 percent.

Student loans are stickier than a mortgage. You can't escape them with bankruptcy, and you may find your wages garnished if you walk away from them, never mind your bad credit rating.

Today, over **40%** **of college grads** end up with a job that ***does not*** require a college degree.

In a speech in mid-2015, Florida Senator Marco Rubio said the rules for colleges' accreditation needed to be loosened for "innovative, low-cost competitors" to succeed. Really? Not sure the facts back up this point of view - especially from a politician who accepted over $27,000 in campaign contributions from Corinthian Colleges and then asked the Department of Education for leniency by not halting federal aid while the company was being investigated.

Oversight is crucial. The presence of the six major college accreditors is supposed to ensure that colleges are doing their job. They are also supposed to evaluate colleges to assist in the determination of which colleges deserve federal funds. However, even the accreditation organizations have become part of the problem. In a recent Wall Street Journal report, it was found that accreditors have grown increasingly more lenient with their evaluations of schools. A recent 2014 report found that out of the 1,500 currently operating accredited four-year colleges, 350 have experienced lower graduation rates than the average college that the same accreditors would have banished back in 2000.

College is important. However, we must make sure that the colleges that are succeeding in their job preparing students — receive the majority of funding. No longer can we afford to fund academic institutions that are not passing the test.

It is the job of our lawmakers to create and sustain an environment where colleges and corporations act in the best interest of the people that trust in them.

THE PLAN

How do we fix this thing?

That's the big question, right?

With so many groups with so many different agendas, how do we make sure that the primary goal is achieved? And that goal is to make sure that every person willing to work hard gets the training they deserve.

And by that I mean every person who puts in the work. Who attends the classes. Who shows up on time. Who stays late. Who's coachable. Motivated. They deserve training as part of their contract with their employer.

Here are the steps we have to take.

#1 - Tie Funding to Results

We have to tie funding to several key indicators and ensure that the money universities receive comes with strings attached. Bright, neon, string, like the rope that you use to tie a cruise ship to a dock.

Funding should be tied to the following success indicators:

1. Graduation Rates
2. Student Debt
3. Income Post-Graduation (Job Placement)

Some will say these numbers are hard to accurately measure, but the facts and realities I have shared to this point will be enough motivation to find a way.

Universities able to prove their graduates receive placement and get the jobs they are promised - should go to the front of the line for funding.

Look at Corinthian College, shutdown for lying to prospective students and their parents about job placement. What does that say about the current thought process of colleges that are fighting to sell degrees? It says we have some bad apples, and we need to find them and stop bankrolling their educational experiment. Just like in business, these colleges should learn from the realities that their students will face when they become workers. If they cannot deliver on the promise that they make, they should fail. We need to shutdown the colleges that are not delivering in the market, and ensure that we reward the ones that are innovating and working to really help prepare their students.

And if the government won't shut them down the students need to. University of Phoenix , a major for-profit company that sells online degrees, has lost 50 percent of its students in the last year. Students have opted out. They aren't showing up to class. And why should they show up to classes that don't deliver on the promises they make?

Tax dollars that go to universities need to be watched more closely for a variety of reasons, and we can no longer blindly trust universities to spend the money they receive wisely. When colleges have more money they spend more money. As college tuition has risen over the last few decades this has been clear by the following fact more than perhaps any other indicator: according to the Department of Education, over the last 10 years the number of administrative employees has grown 50 percent faster than the number of instructors.

In the oversight of our colleges and universities, it is time for us to take attendance. No more passing grades for just showing up.

#2 - Rethink Learning

We must innovate the learning experience, both in the classroom and in corporate training.

The generation entering the workforce is less prepared then ever before. Look closer at the results of the causes of this skills gap and we find opportunities. We learn that it is a generation that grew up playing video games, and it is clear that the way they consume and learn new information has changed. Today, the average millennial will have spent more than 10,000 hours playing games before the age of 21, and at the same time has an average attention span that is less than 8 minutes.

To reach these students, we must engage new learning tools and methods to ensure that the classroom provides the best learning experience possible. We must measure learning and its outcomes to ensure that the content students are taught is retained. The days of data dumping and cramming and forgetting are no longer acceptable if the true goal is to prepare people for the workforce.

The average millenial will have spent **10,000 hours** on a gaming platform by the age of **21**.

There are leading universities and companies that are meeting this challenge to modify the learning experience. I have seen a movement to adjust curriculum to more hands-on and practical training scenarios, and the introduction of gaming platforms to make the training experience more interactive, fun & competitive. With over 90% of classroom based training programs yielding results lasting under 90 days, we must move away from teaching at people, and in turn find better ways to engage people in the learning process.

In a corporate environment, training cannot merely be a line item and a checked box for HR. It must be an ongoing commitment to development. It is no different than situations in sports where an athlete may happen to step on the field without the necessary equipment. In today's workforce, if an employee steps on the field without the tools needed to succeed they get hurt. Their pain is suffered in the form of sub-par performance, sub-par compensation, and ultimately, unemployment.

The worst thing is that entry-level candidates, college interns and students are waiting for their careers to start.

We must get people to work.

We need to get people to work faster. We need to get candidates that are in college programs engaged in organizations faster.

We must create an environment where employees - everyone from entry level to veteran workers - get the work experiences they need.

And that work experience is critical to long-term development. The curriculum you are exposed to, the coursework, the experiences, all of it comes to life when you begin to accumulate experiences in the workplace.

We should not be restricting it. We must create opportunities for people to gain the necessary skills and experience needed so when they go on job interviews they never hear, 'You don't have any experience.'

#3 - Listen & React

To understand what matters most we must do a better job at actually measuring the learning that occurs throughout our educational system. From primary to secondary to post-secondary, we must look closer to understand if what we are teaching is working. We should move beyond just checking a box with the reliance on standardized testing to prove improvement.

We should have an approach to learning that values technical experience, as much as our work in a classroom. We need an approach that really focuses on educating, training and developing people.

See the problem today, as mentioned earlier, is we have created a culture in training and education where we teach at people. We fail to engage people in the process. What we have learned is that this has resulted in weaker outcomes. The modern workforce is different then it was 20 years ago. We cannot give students a 1980's education and expect them to be prepared for a 21st Century workforce.

The work to measure outcomes has to start with understanding both what we are teaching and what today's workforce demands of their people. Let's begin by looking at the curriculum taught in university programs.

There is no doubt that curriculum needs to be reassessed. And it needs to be constantly reassessed as the market changes. Unfortunately, the process to do this is rather clunky and not efficient. I have had professors tell me that making any changes to a course or program can feel like attempting to make a U-turn with an aircraft carrier. Doesn't sound so easy.

The notion that it takes years to change a curriculum creates unneeded challenges. It is a problem when the process to change or update curriculum can take years instead of months. It must be faster. It must be easier.

33%
of companies cite
" LACK OF TECHNICAL "
SKILLS AND TRAINING
as the reason for their
labor shortage.

On-site and off-site split learning must be introduced in the academic experience for students. Giving students exposure to real-life workforce situations is a critical part of the learning and development process. In order to do this there must be greater transparency between academia and corporations, as well as between universities and their students. What is taught in the classroom must continually be challenged to ensure that it remains relevant. We must be better at communicating.

Over the last few years I have reviewed all sorts of research studies that have attempted to better understand what skills are needed to succeed in today's workforce. Some that have popped up have focused on items that we can teach, we can improve on and we can respond to. A few are:

- 55% - Require high levels of customer service and English language proficiency.
- 61% - Require high levels of active listening
- 80% - Are in the service sector

Five of the top twelve skills most valued in today's economy are all communications related. And over 33 percent of companies cite 'Lack of Technical Skills/Training' as the reason for their labor shortage.

We can fix this. We can prevent gaps. And shame on us if we don't.

These are skill gaps that are real today. Students need to know what they are so they can fix them. Colleges need to educate students so they can shrink those gaps. And companies need to better communicate what those gaps are.

I had an intern a few semesters ago that, three weeks into the internship, asked what BCC on an e-mail means. This guy was a graduate student at a university that will charge him close to $200,000 over the course of the program, and it's ridiculous he didn't know the answer. If you ask me it is everybody's fault that it happened.

Universities must take ownership. They must stand behind the students that go out into the market and put their diploma on a wall. They stand by the ones that they win with, and they should stand by the ones they may fail with. If marketing departments at universities want to put their star students and their most successful alumni in commercials and on billboards, they must also be prepared to stand up and take responsibility for the ones that don't reach that same achievement level.

#4 - Reward Companies that get it right

The value of training varies greatly across organizations. These points of view usually fall into three categories. Some believe it is important and setup an environment where training happens and people are constantly working to improve. Some know it is important yet only invest in the minimum to simply onboard new employees with no ongoing training. And some do nothing.

The scale at which training varies is a problem. In a post-recession world we see companies respond by cutting budgets in a variety of areas, but unfortunately training and development too often seams to be one of the first.

We need to find ways to reward the companies that are taking action. We should reward the ones investing in their people. And at the same time we must motivate the companies that are not allocating resources to staff training. All companies that hire people to do a job have the responsibility to prepare those people to succeed. It is mandatory. We should not be ok with a corporate community that does not work its hardest to give all of their people a chance to win. Everybody deserves a fair shot. This is especially true when we know that the impact of a well trained, well prepared and well educated worker is improved productivity, an improved customer experience and a happier staff. Think of it like the trickle down training effect.

I believe companies that invest in training should be rewarded. We should reward the ones that choose to invest in staff development workshops, new training technologies, online learning platforms, continuing education events, advancement of their training and development department and so on. And in doing so we are working towards creating an environment where it is main-stream to promote this behavior in order to ensure that organizations do not look down on this expense with the same scrutiny that they view expenses like office supplies.

A tax benefit for businesses that move toward investing in their people is one way forward.

Companies of all sizes should receive support in the form of tax benefits if they are investing in programs and resources to ensure that the people within their organization have the skills to succeed. Now this impact will be positive for large corporations, where in some cases you find companies that already allocate as much as 6% of payroll on staff training programs, but it will be even greater for small businesses. The small businesses that are at the heart of economic growth and play a major part in creating jobs in today's economy. It's these small businesses that often times do not have all the money and resources to invest in training the people they hire. Usually they struggle just to be able to make the hire in the first place, nonetheless have a budget to effectively train them for their job.

I do not believe that all businesses that fail to invest in training do so because they don't want to. Usually it is a matter of dollars and cents. Do we spend money on training or instead do we hire another employee? Do we spend money on training or do we purchase the new piece of equipment that will increase sales? These are tough questions facing business owners today. And we should do our best to make this easier - to mitigate the risk. And to promote an environment where if business owners are being leaders in their community and choosing to invest in their people, they should see a portion of that spend coming back to them. If you ask me, show me two companies with the same number of workers and the same corporate tax rate, and I feel the one that is investing in their people should get a break.

Rewarding companies with tax benefits for investing in training is a start, but we should not forget about doing the same for positive action on hiring and retention. Companies that are creating jobs and bringing on new workers, as well as seeing a high percentage of retention, should also be rewarded. A recent Bloomberg report showed that when comparing two groups of entry-level workers, a group that received training and a group with no training, 41% of the group that received no training had left within a year. This compared with just 12% of the group that received training.

Training is important. Companies are the ones that we trust will do the right thing and invest in their people. Lawmakers and policymakers must take action. They must make it a priority to be creative in finding ways to create a culture in today's corporations where the understanding is that we are all in this together. That we should help each other. And by doing so they let the companies that choose to invest in their people know that they are not doing so without the full support of their public officials.

#5 - Train Everybody

The United States has been under producing college-going workers since 1980. Supply of workers has failed to keep pace with the growing demand in the marketplace, and as a result we have seen a drastic rise in income inequality.

A 2015 report by the Georgetown University Center on Education & the Workforce found that if we added 20 million postsecondary-educated workers to the workforce, income inequality would begin to decline. In order for this to happen students must make better choices regarding the college they attend and those schools selling an empty education need to be shutdown.

The concept of inequality is present not just in the disparity in income or earnings, but also in training. Workers within organizations often-receive very different training experiences based off their role within the company. In some cases we find that revenue generating sales employees receive as much as five times the training that is offered to a front-line employee earning minimum wage. If we are going to solve the problems we have today we are going to have to approach training globally. We need to understand that it is more than likely that the workers who enter our organizations have not received the baseline skills that they deserve from secondary or post-secondary institutions. We must value all employees across our organizations and ensure that all receive the essential training for success.

Another benefit to note - raising the skills of un-skilled workers within a community has been proven to raise those of skilled workers. The social impact across a community is great. People that are trained and then able to do good work and feel good about the work that they do - this is our goal. We know that we live in a time where most people will spend a greater amount of their life at work than with their loved ones. How can we not believe that training is important when we know how great the social impact can be. Imagine the worker who for some reason or another feels depressed because they just can't seem to perform the task at work as well as they should. Think about the impact that has on the community when that person goes home and brings their work with them. We can do better. And we should.

Across the globe

13% of young people (ages 15-24)

were unemployed in 2014.

And we must start training younger. The unemployment problems caused by poor workforce training is not just a local problem - it is global. Global youth unemployment stats are mindboggling, with this group making up nearly 40 percent of the global unemployed. Recent studies show that 13 percent - some 75 million young people ages 15-24 - were unemployed in 2014. And 1 out of every 3 are not in or receiving any education or training. Some 358 million young people are being left behind. This is all shocking. When you look at the state of unemployment with regards to young people it is still part of a bigger challenge we all face today. With the over 201 million that are currently unemployed across the globe, a figure that has risen over 30 million since the global crisis of 2008, we have to be aware of what the end result can be when we fail in helping our people.

Education is the responsibility of a society, and we face some difficult questions. Are we investing where we should? Are we teaching the right things? Do we reach children young enough? How do we ensure everybody gets the training they deserve? Are our young people mortgaging their future in order to pay for their college degree?

The reality is we know the answers. We know how to fix it. We must take action. This is our job.

CONCLUSION

"EVERY GENERATION HAS THEIR CHALLENGE.
AND THINGS CHANGE RAPIDLY,
AND LIFE GETS BETTER IN AN INSTANT."

JON STEWART
COMEDIAN

You know today, leadership is under attack. Good leadership.

With expectations of performance dropping, the motivations of people changing, the way that you coach and develop people, the very nature of it. What makes it great. Is under attack.

We live in a time where leadership is a word that is overused. People are really just passing on the management styles that were impressed upon them. We find ourselves in a time where the challenges we face as a nation and a society are great, and the choices we make will have a real impact on the direction that we go on so many fronts. We need leaders.

Growing up I had the opportunity to play football for a coach who impacted me greatly - Coach G. He was a coach who would always talk about toughness, hard work, and dedication. And if you asked him, when I saw him at an event in which he got inducted into the Chaminade-Madonna High School

Hall of Fame, he described his job as one that consistently demanded greatness.

I grew up loving sports. As a fan, a player, and a coach, I always saw sports as a reflection of life. The battles, the difficulty, the adversity that you went through are exactly what you will face as an adult. It's no wonder that so many management books that adorn the shelves in bookstores comes from former head coaches whose sage advice is sought out by business leaders.

Leaders today, as managers and educators, must demand more. They must demand more of themselves, and they must demand more of those who they lead. They must be tough and make tough decisions and choices about what they teach, about how they can make it harder, not easier. How they can ensure that people are prepared and ready, not just good enough to pass a test. But really ready.

They have to teach discipline, because anything less than an employee's best is unacceptable. A manager who accepts sub-par performance in a staff training workshop, or subpar performance on the job is hurting their people.

They must focus on accountability. These are the hard things. But these are the things that make the best coaches, leaders, managers and educators stand above the rest. The answer is not to automate learning and make it easier. We should be making it harder on our people. The answer is not to avoid the difficult training and one-on-one sessions, but to lean into them. We must demand more. There can be no shortcuts.

A favorite coaching line I heard along the way that has always stuck with me is, "If we continue to do what we've always done then we will continue to get what we've always got." And what we are getting is not working.

You know, I think back to the moments in my playing career, the moments when I had to keep my head up when I wanted to put it down, when I had to stand up when I wanted to just bend over and gasp for air. The moments when I had to tuck my shirt in and set the example and keep it tucked in even when it wasn't the easiest thing to do. The moments when I had to show up early and stay late to get my work done, and finish the job. The moments when I wanted to sleep in but I had to get up and be on time. These were the moments that taught me the most. The hard ones.

I think of the life lessons I've learned from the people that demanded the most of me because I remember those people. I don't remember those who made things easy. I don't remember those who let me get by. I remember those who challenged me. Today, more than ever, the responsibility of educators, trainers, managers and policymakers is to challenge their people. Raise expectation. Demand more. Expect high levels of accountability. Build an environment of working together as a team. Support each other. Help make each other better. Know that we are all in this together, and we have each other's backs.

Because if we don't - we become part of the problem. We are the ones that will be responsible for passing the buck onto the next generation to solve. Because if we don't - we will be contributing to a trend that will cause a negative impact that will ripple through generations.

This is about work. This is about people. This is not easy stuff.

THIS IS OUR JOB!

ACKNOWLEDGEMENTS

This book is not only based on years of experience, but also countless conversations with teachers, managers, students, employees & lawmakers. It would not have been possible without the many relationships, too many to name, that I have connected with over the years as a colleague, manager & friend. Life is a team sport and bringing this project to life is a by-product of a team of friends, family & many concerned about the issues facing our society today. My deepest thanks to: Lisa Ramirez for helping to bring it all together, Ryan Black for your creative spark, my wife Jahmila for her loving critiques, the team at Sales Huddle Group, my family & of course my mother - for making sure I showed up for my education.

ABOUT THE AUTHOR

Sam Caucci has managed and trained sales and leadership teams for publicly held, private sector and franchised companies across the globe.

In 2010, Sam founded Sales Huddle Group, a workforce training & consulting firm. With work delivered across North America, Europe and Asia, Sales Huddle Group has impacted people across organizations in a wide array of sectors, with clients that include professional sports teams, pro athlete training facilities, hospitality, retail, government, college/university programs, and more. Applying an innovative approach to better staff training, Sam oversaw the creation of The Training Game, a game based training platform that is transforming the way organizations develop their people.

He has been featured on CNN, Fox News, Fox Business, The Wall Street Journal, Bloomberg, ESPN & The Huffington Post.

He lives in New Jersey.

CONNECT WITH SAM

For more information, or to book Sam as a speaker, go to:

Twitter: @samcaucci

Email: scaucci@thesaleshuddle.com

Web: http://samcaucci.com/

Web: www.saleshuddlegroup.com

Or to learn more about The Training Game platform for your team go to:

Web: http://traininggame.saleshuddlegroup.com

Made in the USA
Charleston, SC
20 December 2015